DOGS SET VI

MINIATURE SCHNAUZERS

Nancy Furstinger
ABDO Publishing Company

visit us at
www.abdopub.com

Published by ABDO Publishing Company, 4940 Viking Drive, Edina, Minnesota 55435. Copyright © 2006 by Abdo Consulting Group, Inc. International copyrights reserved in all countries. No part of this book may be reproduced in any form without written permission from the publisher. The Checkerboard Library™ is a trademark and logo of ABDO Publishing Company.

Printed in the United States.

Cover Photo: Index Stock
Interior Photos: Animals Animals pp. 19, 21; AP/Wide World p. 17; Corbis pp. 5, 7, 8, 9, 11, 13, 15, 18

Series Coordinator: Megan M. Gunderson
Editors: Megan M. Gunderson, Stephanie Hedlund
Art Direction: Neil Klinepier

Library of Congress Cataloging-in-Publication Data

Furstinger, Nancy.
   Miniature schnauzers / Nancy Furstinger.
     p. cm. -- (Dogs. Set VI)
   Includes bibliographical references and index.
   ISBN 1-59679-274-4
    1. Miniature schnauzer--Juvenile literature. I. Title.

SF429.M58F87 2005
636.755--dc22

                                        2005043276

CONTENTS

THE DOG FAMILY

Dogs were among the first animals that humans tamed. More than 12,000 years ago, people tamed the friendliest wolf pups as pets, hunters, and guards.

These wolf pups developed into **domestic** dogs. Today, dogs have become our best friends. Almost 400 different **breeds** of dogs exist worldwide. Many have been bred for a special purpose, such as pulling carts or herding cattle.

Dogs vary in color, shape, and size. Yet, they all belong to the Canidae **family**. This name comes from the Latin word *canis*, meaning "dog."

The Canidae family includes wolves, as well as coyotes, foxes, and jackals. Dogs and wolves still

These young foxes do not look very much like miniature schnauzers. But, they are part of the same family.

share **traits**. They howl and growl to communicate. They mark their territory. And, they have good senses of smell and hearing.

MINIATURE SCHNAUZERS

Paintings of schnauzer dogs date back to the 1400s. This **breed** developed in Germany. *Schnauzer* is German for "snout."

The first schnauzers were bred by crossing black poodles and gray wolf spitz with wirehaired pinschers. They herded cattle, guarded farms, and caught rats. These standard schnauzers were crossed with other dogs to create different sizes.

The miniature schnauzer was bred by crossing standard schnauzers with tiny affenpinschers. It started as a ratter, or an animal that catches rats. But, it quickly found favor as a house pet.

The **breed** was brought to the United States in the 1920s. There, the dogs were known as wirehaired pinschers. In 1926, the miniature schnauzer was recognized by the **American Kennel Club (AKC)**.

This young miniature schnauzer is just beginning to show the beard and whiskers typical of the breed. These features usually show up around six to eight weeks of age.

WHAT THEY'RE LIKE

The miniature schnauzer is a small, spunky dog sporting a big-dog personality. If trained properly, they are not timid or shy. And, this **breed** is good with children. They enjoy having fun, and they make amusing playmates!

These active dogs romp in city parks and on country estates. They love to hike, fetch, and swim. They may warn against strangers. But, these friendly dogs will accept new people after checking them out.

A miniature schnauzer is protective of its family.

Miniature schnauzers make friendly pets for people of all ages. They can be very affectionate.

Miniature schnauzers display great intelligence. They are very successful in obedience classes. This is because they are eager to please, and they train easily. Miniature schnauzers can even be trained to carry in the mail or put away their own toys!

COAT AND COLOR

The miniature schnauzer has a double coat. The outer coat is harsh and wiry. It protects a short, thick undercoat.

The **AKC** allows three coat colors. These are solid black, salt-and-pepper, and black and silver. Solid black miniature schnauzers have dark undercoats. But, they may have a small white spot on their chests.

Banded hairs create the salt-and-pepper outer coat. Shades of black and white stripe each hair. The coat appears darker where the hairs are blacker. It fades to a light gray or silvery white on eyebrows, whiskers, cheeks, chest, and legs.

Black and silver coats do not have banded
hairs. Instead, they have black coats with silver
white furnishings. A dog's furnishings are the long
hairs on the head and tail.

This standard schnauzer's beard and wiry coat are typical of all schnauzers.

SIZE

The miniature schnauzer is a compact **breed**. These dogs range in size from 12 to 14 inches (30 to 36 cm) tall at the shoulders. An adult miniature schnauzer's body is usually as long as it is tall. Its weight ranges from 13 to 15 pounds (6 to 7 kg).

The miniature schnauzer has a square-shaped body. The head is rectangular, and the **muzzle** has a relatively blunt end. Small, dark brown eyes are deep set. These features, along with thick whiskers, add to the overall square shape of the breed.

Owners can influence the look of a miniature schnauzer. Some crop the ears, which gives the ears pointed tips. Uncropped ears are small and fold over in the shape of a V. The miniature schnauzer's **docked** tail is set high and carried upright.

Unlike the AKC, the United Kingdom (UK) allows white miniature schnauzers to participate in dog shows. But, the UK does not allow dogs with cropped ears like this dog has.

CARE

Miniature schnauzers need to be brushed weekly. Owners can use a brush made specifically for dogs with a schnauzer's type of fur. Pet miniature schnauzers can be clipped by a groomer every three months.

The dog's body and facial hair should be clipped. The fur on the eyebrows, beard, ears, and legs can be cut with scissors or clippers. Clipping will make the harsh outer coat softer. But, this is acceptable for miniature schnauzers that are simply kept as pets.

If a miniature schnauzer is going to participate in dog shows, its coat must be stripped, or plucked. This can be done by hand or with a stripping knife. Stripping helps maintain the dog's shape as well as the wiry outer coat that is desired for show dogs.

Like this dog, miniature schnauzers should be bathed as part of their regular grooming.

Miniature schnauzers also need to visit a veterinarian. The veterinarian can **spay** or **neuter** your pet. And during your pet's yearly appointment, it will receive a health checkup and **vaccines**.

FEEDING

Your new miniature schnauzer will need to be fed upon arriving home. Stay with the same food it has been eating. You can slowly switch to a new dog food if desired.

Feed your pet a food that provides balanced nutrition. A protein source, such as chicken, should be listed as one of the first ingredients. Read the label to match your dog's age and weight with the daily amount of food it should be fed.

Divide this amount into two meals per day. Feed your pet at the same time each morning and evening. And, serve food and fresh water in stainless steel or hard plastic bowls.

Treat your dog to healthy snacks such as dog biscuits. They are often used to reward good behavior. Rubber bones can safely exercise jaws and help keep teeth clean.

Some stores specialize in products just for dogs. This giant schnauzer (right) can enjoy treats as long as they are part of a balanced diet.

THINGS THEY NEED

Miniature schnauzers should get regular exercise, just like their owners!

Miniature schnauzers exhibit an alert spirit. They are lively animals. And, they quickly become faithful family friends.

They thrive on praise. However, this **breed** also has an independent streak. Miniature schnauzers who become bored may bark and seek out their own amusements.

Along with good training, daily exercise stops most miniature schnauzers from getting into mischief. During walks, attach a nylon or leather

It is important to puppy-proof your dog's play area. Make sure there are no plants in your home or yard that could be harmful to your miniature schnauzer.

leash to your dog's collar. And, make sure your pet has an identification tag in case it becomes lost.

After exercise, dogs need a peaceful place to sleep. Put the dog bed in a crate, which acts as a den. The crate can be near family activities, but should be away from too much commotion. A hard, nylon dog toy will keep your pet company.

PUPPIES

Mother miniature schnauzers are **pregnant** for about nine weeks. Small **breeds** usually give birth to an average of one to four puppies in each **litter**.

Puppies are born blind and deaf. They can see and hear after about two weeks. Puppies take their first steps at three weeks. They are usually **weaned** by about seven weeks of age.

The best source for a **purebred** miniature schnauzer is a qualified breeder. A breed rescue or a **Humane Society** may also have miniature schnauzer puppies and older dogs available for adoption.

Puppies can be adopted when they are between 8 and 12 weeks old. Your new puppy will need to see a veterinarian to continue the series of shots it has already started receiving. A healthy miniature schnauzer will live about 12 to 14 years.

When choosing a puppy, pay close attention to its health and its personality. They are equally important!

GLOSSARY

American Kennel Club (AKC) - an organization that
studies and promotes interest in purebred dogs.

breed - a group of animals sharing the same appearance
and characteristics. A breeder is a person who raises
animals. Raising animals is often called breeding them.

dock - to cut the tail of a dog to a shorter length.

domestic - animals that are tame.

family - a group that scientists use to classify similar
plants or animals. It ranks above a genus and below an
order.

Humane Society - an organization that protects and cares
for animals.

litter - all of the puppies born at one time to a mother dog.

muzzle - an animal's nose and jaws.

neuter (NOO-tuhr) - to remove a male animal's
reproductive organs.

pregnant - having one or more babies growing within the body.

purebred - an animal whose parents are both from the same breed.

spay - to remove a female animal's reproductive organs.

trait - a quality that distinguishes one person or group from another.

vaccine (vak-SEEN) - a shot given to animals or humans to prevent them from getting an illness or disease.

wean - to accustom an animal to eat food other than its mother's milk.

WEB SITES

To learn more about miniature schnauzers, visit ABDO Publishing Company on the World Wide Web at **www.abdopub.com**. Web sites about miniature schnauzers are featured on our Book Links page. These links are routinely monitored and updated to provide the most current information available.

INDEX